HOT JOBS IN VIDEO GAMES

cool careers in interactive entertainment

■SCHOLASTIC

New York • Toronto • London • Auckland • Sydney
Mexico City • New Delhi • H

To my children, Joey and Janey, and kids everywhere—may they reach for and realize their dreams with courage and courtesy.

Thanks to everyone who made this book, a most worthy cause, possible. Any mistakes are solely mine.

table of contents

introduction

Have you ever found yourself playing one of your favorite video games and wondered what it was like to make one? Did you ever find yourself immersed in an environment so cool that you thought about it long after you were done playing?

Welcome to the dominant creative medium of the twenty-first century: video games and interactive entertainment!

Whether you like *Mario*, *Madden*, or Master Chief, riffing as a virtual rock star, or getting wild with a Wii, there's no doubt that video games are fun to play, and if you're a creative person who likes using a computer, you may want to consider video games for a career.

Getting a gig in the video games industry does not have to be just a dream, and it requires the same skills that you're learning in school every day, including art, reading, writing, math, and computers.

This book will give you a better understanding of what it takes to create a video game, and highlight a few of the many jobs you can get in the industry. From legendary game creators to people who actually make a living playing video games, this book will give you an insightful introduction to this fascinating and fast-evolving medium.

Making A Game

The production of a video game, going from a simple idea to a finished product on store shelves, is a challenging but rewarding process that can take years. Along the way, many different people and teams develop the project in a progression of stages.

IDEA Usually it all begins when a producer, an executive, a designer, or an artist—good ideas can spring from anyone—comes up with a new game concept or idea and becomes the **champion** of the idea. This initial spark may be a basic story line, scenario, experience, or perhaps a sequel, enhancement, or spin-off of a previous game.

CONCEPT TESTING The champion usually then comes up with a **game pitch document**. The game pitch document outlines the basics of the game along with a few of its unique selling points or features. Depending on the developer, a small team led by the champion is asked to do a prototype for demonstration to see if the concept is viable, or a

6

concept testing company is hired to test and evaluate the game idea. Concept testing, or prototyping, usually happens before any sort of script or backstory, plots, etc., are made, because if the core concept or prototype isn't fun, there's not much sense in developing it further.

GAME DESIGN DOCUMENT

Once a game concept is approved, a **game design document (GDD)**, which includes concept sketches of game characters, levels, enemies, and more, is created. The GDD becomes the bible that will be used to bring the game to life.

CREATIVE DEVELOPMENT

Three-dimensional designs of all the game's characters, items, enemies, and environments are generated on computers so the design team can figure out how they want them to move and act. Typically, concept artists flesh out a character based on collaboration between the artists and designers. Three-dimensional (3-D) modelers then use computers to create the character based on the concept art.

ANIMATION

The art team focuses on specifics like facial features and expressions while a character is speaking, tiny details that take a ton of work to get right. Specialized artists, called animators, either capture and polish **motion capture** or hand-animate frames not easily motion captured by using a more intensive process called **key framing**. Developers then gather and generate a pile of data about the finer points of each character in the game.

Research has to be done on historical games to make sure outfits are correct. Designers will observe athletes, soldiers, or vehicles in motion and attempt to create characters that mimic these actions as accurately as possible.

AUDIO After a script is written and approved, sound effects are compiled and voice actors are hired to create each character—and all of it is digitally recorded for use in the game's programming. Audio specialists also record (or create) sound effects as needed for the game, such as the cheering of a crowd, the growling of animals, the chirping of birds, or the sounds of various guns firing.

PROGRAMMING While developing a cohesive story line and distinctive art is the first step in the game development process, programming code—that is, creating the software instructions to re-create the game on your computer—is perhaps the most difficult and time-consuming step. Programmers need to have a firm grasp of multiple computer programming languages, as well as an understanding of computer logic and mathematics. A base of code, called the **game engine**, is compiled from scratch or tweaked from a previous game to give the programmers a basic toolbox to create a jumping-off point for their specific assignments. Programmers may have hundreds of tasks that can take anywhere from half a day to a few weeks to complete and debug. Some games take three to four years to create! Programmers create 3-D designs of all the backgrounds, cut scenes, characters, level designs, and sound effects, with the goal of combining them into one coherent game experience. This involves a massive, coordinated team effort, as well as the patience to deal with the grind that comes from long hours and painstaking details.

PLAY TESTING When the programming team nears completion of its task and all of the code and content is assembled, the game is tested. There are typically a lot of art, design, and code bugs to iron out at this stage, so playability testers, focus testers, and designers play the game inside and out, looking for any bugs, errors, or glitches. They play the same portions of the game over and over, sometimes for months, looking for the smallest bugs that need to be fixed, then pass along their findings to the programming team for correction. Playability testers are also responsible for giving their opinion of the game, such as whether the control scheme is easy to use and whether the game has the appropriate feel that the designers were aiming for. Once everything noted by the testers is addressed by the programmers, the game is approved by the team leaders and goes into production. (On rare occasions, if the problems are deemed not fixable, a project is canceled.)

PRODUCTION As a game nears completion, a firm release date is set, giving the production staff a final deadline. At this point the marketing and sales teams kick into high gear, hyping the game to retailers, the media, and the public. The game's final code is compiled and burned to a single master disc, which is then used to mass-produce copies of the game. The game disc is inserted into that familiar plastic packaging and is ready for shipping to retailers.

Animation Stations

Kat Curry
character animator, disney online studios
the world of cars online

Job Skills Needed: Drawing; Anatomy; Computers

Kat is a character animator for Disney/Pixar's *The World of Cars Online*. Her job is to make characters come to life by creating performances that seem physically and emotionally believable and entertaining. "I don't make explosions or buildings fall apart," she says, laughing. "That's for the visual effects animators."

With her fascination for the stop-motion creature movies created by Ray Harryhausen, including *Jason and the Argonauts* and *The Beast from 20,000 Fathoms*, it struck Kat that stop-motion animation wasn't so different from playing with her toys in the backyard when she was a kid, bending their arms and legs to make them look like they were walking or acting out scenes. Kat also loved the behind-the-scenes peeks on *The Wonderful World of Disney* every Sunday night. "It was something I looked

fast fact

The first Pixar production to not feature a human being, *Cars*—in both movie and video game form—presented a unique challenge for character animators to create emotion.

fast fact

To accurately reflect lighting conditions on the cars from the background environments, animators on *Cars* used a new technique called ray tracing.

The World of Cars Online is a kid-safe, virtual world based on the animated feature *Cars*. In the game, kids can design their own car characters. Then they interact with all of their favorite cast members.

forward to," she recalls. "They often showed animators at work, and how the movies were made, and I just knew I always wanted to do that."

Her career arc, like many, was not a straightforward path. After attending a four-year college and earning a degree in math, Kat spent many years as a computer graphics programmer and took art classes on the side. She briefly went to a visual effects school where she focused on character-related topics such as rigging, hair and cloth simulation, and animation. It was there, she says, that she "realized [her] true love was animation and not so much the technology part."

While at the effects school, she got her first opportunity working on a Disney project as a character rigger. Riggers (in CGI) make movable skeletons for character models and provide controls for the animator to use. After that, she worked mostly in movies, sometimes doing crowd simulation, rigging, or animation. "I took every opportunity to do character animation

©Disney/Pixar

Racing at the Carburetor Country Speedway in The World of Cars Online.

when it was available, but was glad I had other background skills when it wasn't," she recalls. "And no, you certainly don't need a math degree or [to] know how to program to be an animator. I'm glad I did those things, but there are many different paths to becoming an animator."

She reminds kids that there are many options just in animation alone, so it helps to know what you like. "Not all animation jobs are the same, and some are more technical than others," she says. There is a big difference between traditional cartoon animation and motion capture, which is when multiple sensors are placed on an athlete or soldier to sense motion that is then translated to the on-screen character

(above) Exploring Red Hood Valley in *The World of Cars Online.*
(opposite) Customizing your Car in your garage.

In *The World of Cars Online,* you can trick out and customize your car in a number of ways, and then work your way up from dirt track racing to compete for the Piston Cup.

to animate him or her in a very fluid and lifelike way. "A large percentage of games involve motion capture," she says. "Sometimes you need to do very realistic work, and sometimes very cartoony. It is good to know which you prefer, so it's good to experiment with a lot of different styles and media, including stop-motion, traditional, and flash."

As animation evolves from ink and paper to the computer screen, Kat says the creativity must still come from within. "Technology has made it possible to create any visual image you want. So the real challenge is coming up with a good idea and a great performance. Many people can animate, but not everyone can create

a really cool character. The job market is incredibly competitive and globalized. You need to be a dedicated artist to be doing this for a living. Simply learning a piece of software will not make your career."

Despite the necessity of learning computers, Kat believes that a well-rounded lifestyle and the ability to observe the world around oneself are important pillars of success as well. "Step away from the computer," she advises. "Find other stuff to do in the real world. Not only will you have fun, but it will make you a better animator. And you'll have better stories to tell if you go out into the world and have adventures. Take acting or dance, and take art classes. Develop your own sense of style. Take note of funny or weird things that happen in your life, even if you're waiting in line at the grocery store just observing what other people are doing. You never know where you will find your next great idea."

One of her favorite things to do outside of her job is play

©Disney/Pixar

Fillmore's Fields in *The World of Cars Online*.

sports, such as Ultimate Frisbee. "It gives me a natural sense of weight and timing, confidence, and knowing how to work with a team of people. These things are as critical to being a great animator as anything else."

As for aspiring animators out there, Kat has some words of wisdom: "People in this field come in all shapes and sizes and ages. You may have heard stereotypes about animators being all crazy and extroverted, but that's not the case. Some are quiet and some are nutty. Be who you are and develop your personal interests. It will make your animation more interesting for people to watch." ■

TOW Mater Animation sequence

Football Fantasy

Mike Young
Art Director, EA SPORTS
Madden NFL

EA SPORTS' *Madden* franchise celebrated its twentieth anniversary last year. The game has sold over 75 million copies worldwide, making it the top sports video game franchise. Mike is the art director at EA Tiburon, the studio that makes the *Madden* games, along with *NCAA Football 10*, *Tiger Woods PGA TOUR 10*, and *EA SPORTS MMA*. Today he gets to work on the game he grew up playing.

"When I was five my dad brought home the Intellivision. Ever since then I have loved games," says Mike. "Throughout my childhood I was always playing games and drawing. Since grade school my favorite subject was always art class. I would draw pictures of my favorite sports players like Ozzie Smith, *Star Wars* ships, and cars. When I went off to college at Mizzou [University of Missouri] my dad encouraged me to be a business major. He

21

When legendary coach John Madden lent his name to EA SPORTS' football series, he wanted to make sure the game was an accurate simulation of the sport. After two decades of evolution, the game is more realistic than ever.

thought no one could make a living at art. So for two years I struggled. I just had no interest in my classes. I spent more time playing games than studying, doing just enough to get by. In my third year of college I was able to take an elective class. Naturally, I took drawing. That class was the first time I had any interest in school. I changed my major after that to fine arts. I really took to painting and photography."

Mike transferred to the University of Illinois at Chicago to focus on graphic arts and graduated in 1999 with a degree in electronic visualization, which was a combination of fine arts and technology training. He spent the next year working

a full-time IT job while creating games on his own at night before he got his first break in the games industry at NuFX in Chicago, working on EA SPORTS' *NBA Street* for the PlayStation 2 and Xbox.

"My big break came on a chance meeting on a flight home," explains Mike. "I was reading a game design book and the guy next to me happened to be a programmer at a game studio in town. We hit it off and he helped me get my interview. As part of my interview I needed to build a VW Beetle in 3-D in less than one thousand polygons. I had a week to complete the test, but I didn't have a 3-D program. I really wanted this jobk so I charged $1,000 that I didn't have to buy a student version of 3-D Studio Max. Best risk I ever took. The test went well enough, and luckily they took a chance on me."

Mike started as an environment artist, building, texturing, and lighting 5 of the 12 courts in the first *NBA Street* game. By

❝ Throughout my childhood I was always playing games and drawing. Since grade school my favorite subject was always art class. ❞

the fourth *NBA Street*, he had worked his way up to become the art director. When an opportunity opened in Orlando to work on the *Madden NFL 09* game, he took it.

"The art director is in charge of the overall visual appearance and quality of the game," explains Mike, who oversees a team of 20 at EA Tiburon. "We are responsible for lighting, cameras, characters, environments, and interface. The art director works with leads in each area to set priorities, define a quality bar, and keep the parts cohesive. In games, the art director works with producers, designers, artists, and programmers to create and execute the visual priorities of the game. One of the most important roles is working with the creative director to make sure the visuals

Madden NFL 10 featured a new design team, tasked with making the game look and feel more realistic than ever. The focus on the simulation aspects of the game added new depth to the series and helped make it the most advanced sports game ever.

❝ Understanding the target audience and being able to solve creative problems are two of the most valuable skills in my job. ❞

Creating realistic weather environments is a tough task for the artists that work on sports games. They must create the appearance of weather like rain and snow, while programmers ensure that the conditions affect the players on the field.

support the overall vision of the game and that the art enhances the game play. Understanding the target audience and being able to solve creative problems are two of the most valuable skills in my job."

Mike says it's been a dream come true working on *Madden NFL 09* and the new *Madden NFL 10*. For him, the best perk of his job is being able to interact with world-class athletes and stand on the sidelines at NFL games. He thinks that

Motion capture technology helps artists build player models around accurate football movements. The animation of human movement is difficult to re-create from scratch, making motion capture an important element of any sports game.

up-close experience helps him create more detailed and impactful graphics. He only wishes he had known earlier in life that a job in games was possible so he could have started working earlier. With all the technology available today, he says that if he were a kid now, he would be making games in his basement with his friends instead of just playing them.

"If you want to be an artist in games, work on the fundamentals first," says Mike. "Anyone can learn software, but the best artists understand the basics. Drawing, painting, sculpture, photography are all great skills that can lead to jobs in games.

Read as much as you can, whether it is a tutorial on building a robot in 3-D [or] a making-of book about your favorite movie. There are also great programs now at colleges that prepare you for working in games. Places like UCF [University of Central Florida] and Carnegie Mellon are just two examples. Find a friend who has similar interests and just start making games. Even if it is just on paper, you can learn a lot and have tons of fun."

Mike says that being good at *Madden* or any other game isn't a requirement for a job in gaming, but loving games is. After all, his team is tasked every year with making a top-10 game with many new innovations. "Living up to that standard is a lot of pressure, but it feels great when you pull it off and millions of people can enjoy the work you did," says Mike. ◼

ratcheting it up

Brian Allgeier
creative director, insomniac games
Ratchet & Clank

Job Skills Needed: Drawing; Programming; Computers

Brian is a creative director at Insomniac Games, the maker of bestselling games like *Ratchet & Clank* and *Resistance*. His first big break in video games was in 1991 as an artist on an interactive CD called *Hanna Barbera's Cartoon Carnival*. Later, Brian shifted his career to game design and contributed level designs on various PlayStation projects, including *Running Wild* and *Spyro: Year of the Dragon*.

In 2001, he became the design director at Insomniac Games and led the design for the first *Ratchet & Clank* game, followed by *Ratchet & Clank: Going Commando* and *Ratchet & Clank: Up Your Arsenal*. As creative director on the *Ratchet & Clank Future* series, Brian oversaw the story, design, and creative direction.

"I've always played games, since I was around ten years old," says Brian. "My brother and I used to play games on Atari 2600

Fast Fact

> ❝ As I was looking to get into different careers, I realized I could combine my interest of art and computers together to make games. ❞

The people tasked with coming up with the art for a sci-fi game like *Ratchet & Clank*, where anything is possible, need to have especially creative minds. The characters and environments must be unique to the series and also reflect the overall design goals of the game.

together, back when characters were just blocky pixels and squares. I enjoyed drawing and I enjoyed programming on a Commodore 64 computer where I created these simple little games. As I was looking to get into different careers, I realized I could combine my interest of art and computers together to make games."

The biggest game creator to influence Brian was Steve Meretzky, who created Infocom's *Planetfall* game. It was an early text-based PC adventure. Brian enjoyed

As video game technology has evolved, the main characters of the series have become more complexly animated and more detailed, letting fans of *Ratchet & Clank* bond with their favorite lombax and robot in new ways with each release.

being able to freely travel through this science fiction world. It included a character named Floyd, and players developed a close connection with this little robot. In fact, Brian found it upsetting when the character died, and that real emotion, even without graphics, inspired Brian to get into games.

Brian went to the Savannah College of Art and Design, where he majored in video and illustration. It was before colleges offered a degree in computers. Ultimately, it was winning a short animated film contest for *Amiga World* magazine that gave him the confidence to move to Los Angeles after graduation.

"I always liked computers, and decided

to move to Los Angeles to try and become an animator," says Brian. "I met Cliff Johnson, who is an author of a popular Macintosh game called *The Fool's Errand*, and he gave me my first real big break in the industry. . . . I really didn't realize at the time that focusing on finishing one piece for my portfolio, a little animated film, [would open so many doors]. Often I would create pieces of artwork and I'd never finish them, and then the one time I actually decided to finish this demo, it really helped my career take off."

As the creative director of the *Ratchet & Clank* game franchise, Brian is in charge of making sure that the vision remains consistent across every department. He's in charge of both the design and the story. He works with the lead designer, the animation team, and the writer to make sure that all the various pieces come together to form a cohesive game. "It really helps to be good at playing games, because when you play them, you really learn a lot," explains Brian. "You learn what other

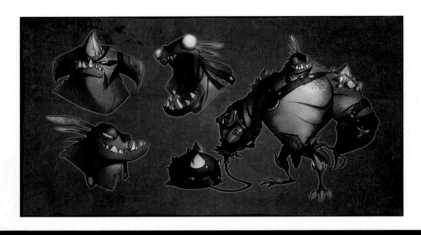

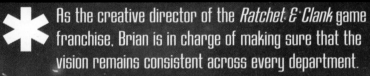
As the creative director of the *Ratchet & Clank* game franchise, Brian is in charge of making sure that the vision remains consistent across every department.

designers and game creators did to make the game fun. You also learn from some of their mistakes. At any point where you're frustrated or confused, you can think of those issues and then try not to make the same mistakes for the game that you're working on."

When it comes to kids who want a cool job in gaming for their own future, Brian says the best way to get into video games is to focus on making a finished project and really work with friends and peers to develop a game.

"I think people can learn a lot about what's involved in working on a team and what each person's role is in the process,

and once you have a finished project, it's something that you can show to another developer, or you can enter it into a contest," says Brian. "You'll get more exposure and people will see you as a game maker and not just a person with random portfolio pieces."

Brian is living his dream, a dream that was born from playing someone else's game a long time ago. Now with the success of *Ratchet & Clank* across PlayStation platforms around the globe, future game creators are being inspired by his work.

"Playing the old text games was great, but I just imagined these places that I was going to and felt like it'd be great if I could actually see some of these worlds and have all the visual and audio that I was imagining in a game," says Brian. "I've fulfilled that dream by developing these science fiction stories in *Ratchet & Clank* and working with a great team to create these amazing, fantastic alien worlds." ■

fast fact

The artists responsible for *Ratchet & Clank* get to see their work in numerous places outside the series. The characters appear as "Easter eggs" in over half a dozen other games and even make an appearance on the poster for the film *Paul Blart: Mall Cop.*

Going Great Guns

Cliff Bleszinski
Creator and Design Director, Epic Games
Unreal, Gears of War

Job Skills Needed: Creativity; Computers; Management

Gamers around the world know the work of Cliff, the creator of Microsoft and Epic Games' bestselling *Gears of War* franchise. In addition to the blockbuster video games, toys, novels, and comic books, there's also a movie in the works from New Line Cinema.

Cliff serves as Epic Games' design director. He's a 17-year veteran of the computer and video game industry. In fact, Cliff shipped his first commercial game, *Jazz Jackrabbit*, before graduating from high school. He continues to lend his creative expertise to Epic's upcoming projects such as *Shadow Complex*, which is based on bestselling author Orson Scott Card's latest novel, *Empire*. Cliff has expanded the scope of his work to include other entertainment sectors as well.

"The first game I ever played was *Space Invaders* on the Atari

With iconic artistic qualities and an epic story line, *Gears of War* was ingeniously designed by Cliff from the ground up to be spun into movies, graphic novels, and the like.

2600," says Cliff. "I was instantly hooked by the idea of manipulating images on my television screen but wasn't quite old enough or aware that this could be a possible career. The title that inspired me the most would have to be the original *Super Mario Bros* on the Nintendo Entertainment System. There was something about these cartoony worlds that unfolded before me that were filled with secrets that, at the time, I believed were not meant to be discovered by the designers."

When he was a kid, Cliff liked to play any and all games that he could get his hands on, including old Nintendo games like *Deadly Towers* and *Athena*. What he

didn't realize at the time was that this was his training for his job today. He eventually got an Apple IIc and Basic and started cranking out Infocom-style text adventure games. He then graduated to an IBM 386 SX and a copy of Visual Basic that he used to start making graphical adventures similar to *Déjà Vu* and *Uninvited*.

"I sold copies of my games out of my mother's house in Ziploc bags around when the CompuServe forums and the shareware industry were in full swing," says Cliff. "I checked out a little game called *Jill of the Jungle* that had a call for talented partners at the end of it. I sent a prototype of my next adventure over to Tim Sweeney and Mark Rein, and within days Mark called me to gush about how cool my game was, and he pitched all sorts of ideas for improvements, which terrified my then seventeen-year-old self. Luckily, he didn't scare me away. I later partnered with them to build *Jazz Jackrabbit* and eventually went on to *Unreal* and *Unreal Tournament*."

As Epic's design director, Cliff contributes to the creative process for all of the company's games and related media. He spends a lot of time developing the *Gears of War* universe by figuring out what new elements to add while staying true to the series, testing new content for *Gears of War 2*, and also working on secret, unannounced projects.

"Games generally start out as high-level concepts," explains Cliff. "Once a team drafts the initial design treatment, the game moves into preproduction and prototyping. At Epic, we use tools like Unreal Kismet to mock up potential enemies and weapons, for example. Once you start building out the world, you have to figure out the core game-play loop, which is the basic idea behind the game that makes it fun. During production, you also have to decide what features are essential to making your game fun, cut nonessential 'like-to-have' items, and polish, polish, polish. Iteration and great user feedback is key to making a good game."

fast fact

Because it was built on the *Unreal 3* game engine, *Gears of War* required only 20–30 people working on it full-time This base code allowed the design team to focus on how to make the game cooler than ever without having to build a new engine from scratch.

Epic Games also creates the technology, called Unreal Engine 3, that powers games such as Sony Online Entertainment's *DC Universe Online* and 2K Games' *Bioshock 2*. "A game engine is a complex piece of software on top of which you build your game, and it ties together key systems like rendering, physics, animation, audio, networking code, artificial intelligence," Cliff explains. Epic continually makes improvements to the Unreal Engine and is a big supporter of game developers everywhere.

Cliff says that for a career in video games, playing games is important, although he likes to think that a variety of life experiences and cultural references are the best grist for the mill. Inspiration can come from so many places—random dreams, graphic novels, socializing with friends, amazing road trips—that you never know when or where a cool idea will surface. He thinks it's important to surround yourself with as many pop culture and literary influences as possible, because that will ultimately make you a better game designer.

" " I was instantly hooked by the idea of manipulating images on my television screen. . . . The title that inspired me the most would have to be the original *Super Mario Bros.* **" "**

No game happens without inspiration, and Cliff credits the games that helped spark him to create the spectacular *Gears of War: Kill Switch* and *Resident Evil 4* helped inform the design and game play of the series, while *Bionic Commando* influenced the movement and motion.

"Getting into games takes a lot of hard work, a lot of talent, and also a bit of luck," Cliff says. "If you're more of an artist you should acquire as much traditional training as you can and then move on to creating digital works. If you're more math and problem-solving oriented you should look into learning various programming languages."

He continues, "Ultimately, succeeding in games will require a lot of trial and error. You have to be willing to throw away the

first thousand images you create. Your portfolio is only as strong as your weakest link. You need to network online and eventually get to the Game Developers Conference, show up with copies of your work, and get feedback from professionals firsthand." Cliff thinks the games industry is very accessible and most industry pros are friendly. "If you are a hard worker with talent, you will catch their attention. You just have to make sure your work and ideas get into the right hands. You can do that by posting your samples online or attending special gaming conferences in your area," he says.

"Mod making [creating new levels or variations on an existing game] is another great way to get started in the business," adds Cliff. "A significant number of Epic employees got started in the mod community, and now they're living the dream of making triple-A [blockbuster] titles." ■

Art Simulates Life

Will Wright
creator, stupid fun club
the sims; spore

Job Skills Needed: Computers; Creativity

Will first became a big name in gaming when he developed *SimCity*, the acclaimed, nonviolent, open-ended simulation game. Will followed up the success of *SimCity* with a string of popular simulation games throughout the 1990s. Titles such as *SimEarth: The Living Planet* (1990), *SimAnt: The Electronic Ant Colony* (1991), *SimCity 2000* (1993), *SimCopter* (1996), and *SimCity 3000* (1999) introduced simulation games to hundreds of thousands of new fans, demonstrating the genre's potential.

Will's next groundbreaking game was *The Sims* (2000), which has gone on to become the bestselling PC game franchise of all time and is now available in 22 languages in 60 countries. Will, who studied architecture in college, originally created the software to help architects design buildings. To "score" the quality of the design, he added tiny people who would inhabit the buildings.

Johnny
Listen
Acquaintance

§5.670

With a string of hit titles including *The Sims* and now *Spore,* Will uses his platform as a successful game designer to encourage aspiring designers to let their minds wander and take risks with their concepts.

These simulated people quickly stole the spotlight, and Will realized that watching the lives of these Sims unfold was the real entertainment. *The Sims* franchise has gone on to sell more than 100 million units worldwide.

Widely acknowledged for creating the simulation genre, Will unveiled *Spore* in 2008. *Spore* allows players to create a species, help it build a society, develop its culture, and explore an infinite cosmos of worlds created by other players. *Spore* has been distinguished with such honors as *Popular Science*'s Best of What's New

Award, *Popular Mechanics'* Breakthrough Award, *PC Magazine's* Technical Excellence Award, and the Jim Henson Technology Honor. *Rolling Stone* named Will one of the 100 People Who Are Changing America in March 2009, which placed him among artists, leaders, scientists, and policy makers who are "fighting every day to show us what is possible."

Will credits his passion for models as a kid for getting him into games. "I always liked games as a kid, and I always liked making models," Will recalls. "And my model making slowly evolved into building robots—things with motors that would drive around. I bought my first computer to control my robots and ended up teaching myself to program, and in doing that I started learning about things like artificial intelligence and simulation and started realizing that I could build little simulations on the computer."

In many ways, that idea of creating an environment in a game continues today. "The best examples of those worlds, at the time and even now, are games where the players are making these little simulated worlds, which, in some sense, is a form of modeling."

Will considers this combination of passion and practical experience a key to his success. "When I would build models, I would always build models of things that interested me. I was very interested in military history and aviation and space life and things like that. And in building a model, I found that I was just kind of naturally learning more about these subjects. And so, on the computer, the same thing happens. When I build a model of the way a city works, I end up researching a lot about cities and their dynamics and behavior. And so modeling, for me, is a great way to learn about something."

But his interests also helped him understand the importance of learning the fundamentals taught in school, now that he had found his ideal outlet to apply them. "For me, I was okay in math. I never really enjoyed it that much. But I'm into building these model worlds, and at some point math became a tool for me. When I realized what I could do with math, it all suddenly became fascinating. It was totally a matter of how relevant it was to what I wanted to do," he says.

In addition to finding ways to build off the basics he learned in class, Will also feels the school of hard knocks was an important part of his learning process. "I see the entire path I've taken as a learning experience, and I'm not sure I could really short-circuit that and take something that I had learned years later and bring it [back] in time. I don't think it would have had that much

> **One of the things I would definitely not want to do is go back in time and tell myself, 'Don't do this. It's gonna fail,' because I would've basically avoided a very deep learning experience.**

Will believes that learning and being creative is a lifetime process, and that there is no substitute for getting out in the world and expanding one's horizons.

meaning for me at that point. I probably would not have listened to myself from the future."

As in a linear role-playing game (RPG), where the hero has to perform specific tasks in sequence to advance, Will still considers himself a student. "I had to slowly build up my experience. So just the process of me going through my career and doing things I've done, I've learned probably more from my failures than

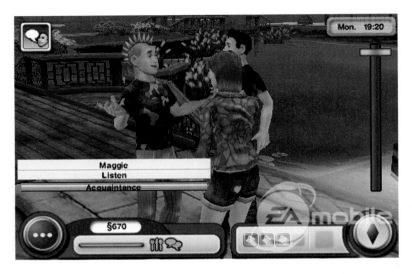

Will is back doing what he loves most and does best: creating truly unique games and interactive experiences. His new development company, Stupid Fun Club, is cooking up all sorts of cool projects you will be hearing more about soon.

I have my successes. One of the things I would definitely not want to do is go back in time and tell myself, 'Don't do this. It's gonna fail,' because I would've basically avoided a very deep learning experience."

Will thinks that "the most important skill, by far, and, in fact, it's more than a skill" is "to develop an appreciation for how fun learning can be." He says, "A lot of times, people, especially kids, associate learning with sitting in school for hours on end and being bored. But most of the effective learning that I've had in my lifetime was stuff that I wanted to learn, and I went out and learned on my own.

"Teachers can help you and guide you and give you background and maybe even introduce you to things that you normally wouldn't trip across, but I think from a kid or adult's point of view, I think the primary thing that I've come away with is that you need to take responsibility for your own education. Don't just sit in class for eight hours a day assuming you're going to automatically find something that motivates or inspires you."

Will concludes, "I think the best advice is to find something you love doing, and if you love doing it, you'll do well, and if you don't really enjoy what you're doing, you're not going to do it as well, no matter how hard you try." ■

A Raging Good Time

Matt Hooper
Game Designer, id Software
DOOM 3

Matt is a game designer who has been creating games professionally since 1996. Currently, as id Software's lead designer on the multiplatform action title *Rage*, he provides direction for the design team. Matt started his career working as a contract designer for the *Quake Mission Pack #1* with Ritual Entertainment. During his 10-year career he's worked on more than 10 titles, most recently as designer on the award-winning *Doom 3* and as executive producer on the *Doom 3* expansion *Resurrection of Evil*.

His entry into the industry wasn't inspired by any one game or moment. "You could say the industry itself was my inspiration," he says. "I grew up as personal computing grew up and video games as an extension went along for the ride. I can still remember winning an award in my sixth-grade drama class; the

fast fact

The first title to feature id's new id Tech 5 engine, *Rage*'s underlying base was created with designers in mind: The goal is to make the engine easier to develop for than previous id creations.

Times are busy at id, with new titles like *Rage* and *Doom 4* putting the company back in the spotlight. Published by Electronic Arts, *Rage* has it all: unique game play, killer design, and the marketing muscle to stand out from the crowd.

contest was to act out targeted future careers using no props or sounds. As a shy kid it took a bit of courage to get up onstage and pretend to hold an Atari 2600 controller and play games, but it worked. My thirst for all things related to computers and gaming was intense throughout those years, and this put me on a direct course into the industry."

As the interactive entertainment and video game industry has matured, so have the career paths. When Matt began, "everything was driven almost solely on passion, whereas now you'll find many higher learning institutions offering industry-focused choices in their curriculum."

"Making a buck in my early years was an afterthought," he says. "Instead, what I craved most was fan and peer recognition. My career started getting interesting after creating virtual worlds in the *Wolf 3D* and *Doom* engines. At this point the Internet was coming alive and creating an outlet to share my creations. Compilations, which included my work, were showing up on store shelves."

Matt believes creating modifications for existing software was and probably still is one of the best ways to sharpen skills. Plus, cool modifications can really catch the industry's attention. "I got noticed by a few companies early on through my mod work, eventually accepting my first paying job working as a contractor with Ritual Entertainment on the first *Quake Mission Pack*. Shortly after, I decided to enter the industry full-time by accepting a position at Ion Storm in 1997. Wanting a bit more, I, along with some of my peers, decided to do it on our own, creating Third Law

> **Keep an eye on the crests of the new waves in this industry and if you see one that excites you, jump on it and ride, because having that passion in your work will always take you further than talent alone.**

With a memorable mix of immersive environments and over-the-top characters, *Rage* is a riveting world that keeps gamers coming back for more.

Interactive in late 1998. Co-owning a game company was difficult but a blast. At Third Law we worked on everything, ranging from a game based on the rock band KISS to a mini-golf game to *Aliens vs. Predator* to Disney games. As much fun as I was having there, I couldn't resist the offer to come to id Software in 2002 to work on *Doom 3*, and I've been here ever since."

His first big break at id came when John Carmack released a format for creating

mods (see page 50) in the *Quake* engine before the game was released. "At first glance this may not seem like a break, but it gave me the ability to create 3-D worlds using only a text editor when most people were not even aware this was possible," Matt recalls. "That got me noticed in a big way and eventually led to my entry into the industry."

Matt's advice for kids today is to "keep an eye on the crests of the new waves in this industry and if you see one that excites you, jump on it and ride, because having that passion in your work will always take you further than talent alone. I'm noticing that I put more and more emphasis on things like work ethic, passion, and attitude when hiring. So while your portfolio may look great, it's been my experience that those intangibles are what make the really great teammates." ■

MUSIC MAKERS

David Iscove
Audio Assets Specialist, Activision
Guitar Hero

Job Skills Needed: Music; Computers

When it comes to music video games, *Guitar Hero* is the title that created the genre. With Activision working on *Guitar Hero 5*, *Band Hero*, and *Guitar Hero Van Halen*, there's plenty of new music to come. David is an audio assets specialist for the *Guitar Hero* franchise.

"[For] a musician and a music lover, *Guitar Hero* is the perfect spot between listening to my favorite music and playing video games," says David. "For me, it's the best of both worlds."

Musically, David listened to a combination of heavy metal and pop music like *Appetite for Destruction* by Guns N' Roses and . . . *And Justice for All* by Metallica, which he says changed his life forever.

David went to school in Boston at Berklee College of Music, played guitar in several bands, and did recording sessions for

72

Did you know?

Activision has sold more than 25 million copies of the five games and numerous spin-offs in the *Guitar Hero* franchise, one of the best-selling series in video game history.

fast fact

Though the first games in the series featured few songs by original artists, rock stars now line up to have their songs featured in *Guitar Hero*. Artists often have to help with the remastering of their original music tracks into the proper format for the game, if they want to become part of the legendary series.

> ❝ Once a song is licensed, or approved to be used in the game, I work with the artist or label to format their original multitrack recordings into a way that the game handles audio. ❞

friends. From there, he started working for film composers, where he learned the world of audio production in film, television, and video games.

"The video game scores that I did with those composers were more fun and smooth to work on than any of the films or television shows we did, so I thought there was something about the video game industry that made it different," explains David. "The video game companies we were hired by had a confidence about themselves that no other industry had. It made me want to explore it more. I applied for a note-tracking position at one of the developers of *Guitar Hero* based on my knowledge of MIDI [musical instrument digital interface], and instead of getting that job, I ended up at the parent company, Activision."

David grew up playing games. He had all of the systems as a kid, from Intellivision to the Nintendo Entertainment System, which he used to play games like *Super Mario Bros.*, *Duck Hunt*, and *Shark Shark*. Back in those days, neighborhood arcades were still around, and he plugged plenty of quarters into games like *Donkey Kong* and *Spy Hunter*.

In his current role as audio assets specialist, "I oversee the delivery of stem mixes," says David. "That means that once a song is licensed, or approved to be used in the game, I work with the artist or label to format their original multitrack recordings into a way that the game handles audio."

With support for a band of four, *Guitar Hero* now allows players to come within a stone's throw of being real rockers. Drum parts are the most accurately transcribed, while playing guitar and singing require timing and talent.

David explains, "We take each part of a song and try to interpret how it would be played on our controllers. For drums, we can be perfectly accurate (playing expert drums on *Guitar Hero* is an exact transcription of the real thing). For other instruments that have fewer buttons than the original instrument has notes, we have to limit or interpret how that would seem. The rule of thumb is, if a song has more complicated riffs, faster parts, and doesn't repeat too much, it will be more fun to play in the game."

David says being good at *Guitar Hero* is important for his job. "You have to be good at the game to show artists how to play and to make them excited enough to want to be

in the game themselves," he says. "When you're demo-ing the game for a rock star, you definitely don't want to fail out."

Although he has to work on all of those *Guitar Hero* songs, when asked to choose a favorite, David chose "Shortest Straw" on *Guitar Hero Metallica*. He says the band doesn't play it much live anymore, so he was psyched that they were cool with putting it into the game.

When it comes to the latest in video game music, David says playing it with surround sound speakers is awesome because it puts the player inside the game experience sonically and increases the realism. He notes that if you're only using your TV speakers, you're missing a big part of what makes music games so uniquely fun to play.

As for aspiring game rockers, David has some advice: "Play as many games as possible and the types that you love. Once you've determined what your favorite style is, learn as much as possible about the people and company that made the game. See

if there's anything you can do to intern or be involved with them. Once you get in the door, work hard to establish a reputation as someone who is reliable and can be counted on to get the job done. There's nothing more satisfying than being involved in creating a product that you would buy yourself."

Future *Guitar Hero* game creators have an advantage over David because so much more music technology is available at their fingertips. He says the days of old recording studios that were off-limits to anyone who didn't have a big budget are gone. Kids can make music at home and even program code to create their own games and animation, so his advice? "Start teaching yourself!" ■

fast fact

Music games have reached a whole new group of people who might not have played video games before, and it's easy to see why: With artists ranging from Taylor Swift to Metallica, from Johnny Cash to Kurt Cobain, there is certainly something for everyone.

Paid to play

Johnathan "Fatal1ty" Wendel
professional video gamer

Job Skills Needed: Hand-eye coordination; Reflexes; Determination

Ever wish you could play video games for a living? Today there's actually a career for professional gamers, thanks to global video game leagues like Major League Gaming. One of the first professional gamers to rise through the ranks in America was Johnathan, best known as "Fatal1ty" to opponents and fans alike. Wendel has won 12 world titles in five different games and is the most recognizable face in e-sports today. In 2007, he was presented with the first Lifetime Achievement Award in the history of pro gaming.

Back in 1999, Johnathan became the first professional gamer in the United States. After winning $4,000 in his first PC gaming tournament in Dallas, Texas, Johnathan traveled from tournament to competition around the globe full-time, playing id Software's *Quake* for cash and prizes. He traversed five continents in his first

Johnathan has won more than $500,000 playing in video game tournaments over the years, including a $150,000 check for winning a world championship.

Though formal e-sports events have grown in popularity over the years, competing for money through games is no new concept: The idea dates back to some of the first titles ever released in arcades.

year as a pro, racking up wins all along the way.

"No one was really making a living playing video games," says Johnathan. "There was some money to be won, just not full-time money. It eventually picked up to where it became a definite possibility, so I took advantage of the situation and ended up winning over $100,000 my first year as a pro."

Johnathan played sports throughout school and did pretty well in traditional

classes while excelling at math. All during high school, he gamed on the side and competed in small tournaments.

"When I graduated from high school, I realized there were tournaments offering big money for the game I was super passionate about," explains Johnathan. "One of the guys I trained with won a big tourney in Europe, so that's when I realized I had the talent to win. I competed from then through today, and even started a great business making products for gamers around the world, working with Creative, XFX, and OCZ. So now I work pretty hard with the companies that develop new Fatal1ty Brand products, everything from headphones [to memory], power supplies, graphic cards, and sound cards."

Johnathan has won more than $500,000 playing in video game tournaments over the years, including a $150,000 check for taking home the top prize in the 2005 CPL World Championship. Today he spends a lot of his time running Fatal1ty Inc., which makes new video game products to help other gamers become better at competitions.

"I realized I needed different equipment than what was being offered to step up my game to the next level, so I decided to start designing and making my own products," says Johnathan. "Eventually, it turned into a very successful business that helps gamers all around the world play at the highest level."

Gaming remains a big part of Johnathan's life. He spends four to eight hours a day playing games. He loves the experience and the competition of playing the best players around the world from the comfort of his own home. He says that like American gamers, the Europeans are great competitors, especially gamers from countries like Sweden and Finland.

"Obviously, console gaming has done well and more people are getting into gaming through Wii, but to be on the cutting edge of gaming, the PC is always the first one to have anything," says Johnathan. "Look at *World of Warcraft*. It's one of the most popular games in the world, and it's only available on the PC. I'm also a big fan of the Xbox 360 and Nintendo Wii, but when

it comes to playing first-person shooters or being more enticed to my game where I want to do something different, I love the PC for that. The quality of graphics and sound are ten times better than the console."

Although he took an unconventional path, Johnathan says there are a million ways to get into the gaming business, from programming to art to marketing and every other possibility.

"Just find out what you would love to do, and in gaming you'll most likely find that job," said Johnathan. "Kids today are more hardwired than ever before. I was lucky to see computers still booming, so I know exactly how a PC works and how all the code affects the program or game. I feel young kids today, though, have a huge advantage in technology over the generation I grew up with."

When he's not working or practicing, Johnathan likes to keep competitive, playing real sports and card games. ■

COMIC BOOK HERO

Chris Baker
Manager of Licensed Games, Marvel

Job Skills Needed: Reading; Research; Communication

As Marvel's manager of licensed games, Chris works on what's known as "brand assurance" for all Marvel video games, which means he has to make sure that everything created for Marvel video games is true to form in every respect. Marvel has licensing agreements with companies such as Activision (Spider-Man, X-Men), SEGA (Iron Man), and THQ (Super Hero Squad), and all of these companies create and publish games with Marvel's guidance.

It's Chris's job to make sure every facet of Marvel games—everything from when a game is just an idea on a sheet of paper to when it has become a fully packaged item you buy in the store—lives up to Marvel's standards. If it doesn't, he'll provide feedback to the publisher on how to make things better, and the developers do their best to address Marvel's comments.

Ever since making his first appearance in a Marvel comic book in 1962, the Incredible Hulk has always been a hit with gamers. His meanness and greenness have made his character a smash to play on many systems through the years.

In order to fulfill this goal, there are a lot of things Chris is responsible for. First of all, he's reading, writing, and responding to e-mails pretty much all day; communicating with the publishers and other Marvel employees is probably the most important part of his job. He also spends a lot of time doing research, which means lots of playing games and reading comics. He has to review plot ideas and art samples, and give input on characters and settings. Chris has to know the Marvel brands inside and out and be an expert on what the characters would and wouldn't do, and what can and cannot happen, in their world.

Chris got his start writing for a

gaming website his senior year in college. He majored in communications with a focus on advertising. "A major like that helped me hone my writing and creative skills, which came in very handy for my writing career to follow," Chris says.

After he freelanced for the website for about 18 months, writing about literally hundreds of games, his experience led to a job working at the *Official U.S. PlayStation Magazine*, right before the PS2 came out. "Getting to see games early and preview—even review—them for the world was an amazing experience," Chris recalls. "But in 2005, I decided to accept a public relations job with LucasArts, which meant I got to work with *Star Wars* on games like *Battlefront II* and *LEGO Star Wars II*. After a couple of years there, though, it became clear to me that I actually wanted to work more closely on the games, not just tell people why they're great, as a PR person does. So when the opportunity at Marvel came along in 2007, I couldn't pass it up."

fast fact

While much of the game reflects the story line from the movie, *X-Men Origins: Wolverine* builds on the film's plot and includes events and sequences unique to the interactive experience.

> **There's a lot you can be doing at your age to put yourself in a good position for a career in video games, especially now with the power of the Internet.**

Despite his amazing success, Chris thinks it might have helped if he had worked harder early on to get a job in the industry. But he also feels that "anyone anywhere can get involved. Growing up in Memphis, Tennessee, there wasn't much game development or anything like that nearby, so I didn't really even consider the industry as an option until well into college. I feel incredibly fortunate for things to have progressed as they did for me, but I can only imagine I would have had an easier time if I had begun setting myself up for a career in the industry before high school."

To grade school kids, Chris advises, "There's a lot you can be doing at your age to put yourself in a good position for a career in

Did you know?

With a history stretching back to 1939, Marvel has a treasure trove of characters that have provided great starting points for many fun video games through the years.

Video games have enabled generations of fans who first read about their favorite superheroes in comic books, then watched them in television series and major motion pictures, to finally play them in all sorts of cool scenarios.

video games, especially now with the power of the Internet. If writing about games is something you want to do, then start making yourself known on message boards and blogs—maybe even create your own website or write a column for your school or town newspaper. If making games interests you, there are a ton of great books that can inform you about everything from production work to programming. When you're old enough, you might even want to get a job as a tester in quality assurance if there happens to be a game publisher near you."

Chris's firmest advice is to work hard and play hard. "No matter what you want

to do in the industry, keep playing games," he says. "If you're serious about it, the very act of playing games—thinking about what makes them good or lousy—is every bit as worthwhile as reading a book or playing outside, though don't forget to do those activities, too!"

He also feels we're still just at the beginning of a very long growth curve for interactive entertainment. "Games are still very young as a medium," Chris says, "and before you know it, the games of the future will make *Call of Duty* and *Gears of War* look like the original *Frogger* and *Donkey Kong* by comparison. Games just won't look better; they'll be entertaining us in ways we can only—maybe even *can't*—imagine. And guess what: *You* reading this book could be the one who changes everything." ∎

Imagining Mayhem

Joshua Ortega
Game scriptwriter

Joshua's work spans nearly the entire spectrum of the popular arts. He has written for every major American comic book company, including Marvel, DC Comics, Dark Horse, Image, and more, working on high-profile properties such as *Star Wars*, *Spider-Man*, *Star Trek*, *Frank Frazetta's Death Dealer*, and *Battlestar Galactica*.

A former journalist, Joshua is also the author of a wide variety of Xbox 360 titles for Microsoft Game Studios, including the bestselling smash hit *Gears of War 2*. He has been featured numerous times on National Public Radio and has also appeared on the Sci Fi Channel, FOX TV, G4, and XPlay, in addition to many other major media outlets.

He was drawn to video games by his fascination with the

❝❝ This industry is changing the world, and I'm very proud to be a part of it. As we joke sometimes, 'Look, Ma, playing all of those games *did* pay off!' **❞❞**

As graphics improve and characters look more realistic all the time, it is critical for the scriptwriters to ensure that the story and depth behind each character evolve as well.

interactive screen. "Video games, interactive entertainment, dynamic storytelling, whatever term we use to describe this medium, I'm just really excited that we're finally being recognized as a legitimate art form," he said. "I think we, as gamers, have always known this on an intuitive level. But now we're the major art form, we're pushing the boundaries of storytelling and art, of design and technology, and it's just a fantastic place

❝❝ When everyone is synced up and working together, you can put out an amazing piece of art and an amazing product that satisfies the needs of the publisher, [the] developer, and the people who play. **❞❞**

to be. This industry is changing the world, and I'm very proud to be a part of it. As we joke sometimes, 'Look, Ma, playing all of those games *did* pay off!'"

Joshua took a typically atypical path to the industry, attending college but not graduating. Instead, he focused on honing his skills and pursuing his passion, which he admits may not be the best route for everyone.

His first big break in the industry came when his novel *((Frequencies))*, comics, and graphic novels gained notoriety. "That really paved the way for my work in the games industry. By proving myself in other media, it allowed me to work on

fast fact

No longer can a game succeed with bland, generic characters—even if they look really cool. Games need good storytellers to add insight and emotion to the splashiest of graphics and most excessive of explosions.

A big challenge of writing for a game can be working on sequels. When working on a story someone else started, writers must make sure the new story line faithfully carries on the legacy of the original while providing sensible new depth and detail.

triple-A titles like *Gears of War 2*, *Blue Dragon*, and *Lost Odyssey*.

"If we're talking about specifics, then I'd say my big break was writing the 'bridge' story that connected the *Knights of the Old Republic* for Dark Horse Comics, Lucasfilm, and Bioware. That story really proved to people that I knew games, loved the medium, and was willing to do the research necessary to respect the franchise, continuity, and, most importantly for me, the story."

Joshua believes his ability to fulfill his role as a storyteller, and to be a team player, are the keys to his success. To do his job well, he says a writer needs to

"make sure that he is always synchronized with the developer and designers, is intimately involved with the early stages of level design, and is also collaborating with the other essential parts of the team. When everyone is synced up and working together, you can put out an amazing piece of art and an amazing product that satisfies the needs of the publisher, [the] developer, and the people who play."

He thinks kids should not be afraid to follow their dreams. "It can sound clichéd," he says, "but it's the most important thing you can do in your life. Be prepared for hard work and dedication, and also be prepared for those who will tell you [you] cannot succeed. Don't let them get in your way; they're roadblocks on your life's journey, and you need to steer around them. Only by doing what you love will you truly be able to succeed." ■

writing for Fun & Games

Journalists' Roundtable

we gathered three veteran writers and editors from the world of video games to discuss their corner of the industry and explore how they got where they are. while outsiders may think writing about video games is all fun and games, it's not. with us today are Dean Takahashi, blogger for VentureBeat.com; John Gaudiosi, freelance writer; and Joe Funk, owner and editor at Mojo-Media.com.

First question is obvious: How did you all get started?

John: I've been playing video games since the Sears Pong console, but I never thought it would lead to a career. My parents always yelled at me, telling me I spent too much time playing video games when I was a kid. In college, I became entertainment editor at George Mason University's *Broadside* student newspaper and started writing about games. That opened up a door to the *Washington Post*, which was the first mainstream paper to cover games. From there, I started freelancing for sites like

CNET's GameCenter and *GamePro* magazine. I got a job in San Francisco with *Incite Video Gaming* and *MCV*, and they moved me out west from Washington, D.C. That full-time gig in the heart of video game editorial country is what really sealed the deal for me as far as my career. Currently, I am a freelance writer and travel more than a hundred thousand miles a year covering video games around the world.

Dean: I became a journalist first. I always loved reading, writing, and gaming. I majored in English at the University of California at Berkeley, but even in college I spent too many quarters and too much time in the arcades. I learned firsthand about journalism while working at the Institute for Journalism Education at Berkeley, and then went on to get a master's degree in journalism at Northwestern University. I started work and spent many hours playing games in my free time. But this avocation didn't combine with my vocation for many years. I migrated to covering tech news at the *San Jose Mercury News* in 1994 and have covered tech news in Silicon Valley ever since. In 1996, I started a job in the San Francisco bureau of the *Wall Street Journal.* I was the youngest guy in the office and I inherited the video game beat. I wrote stories where the primary aim was to explain to nongamer adults what their kids were doing. At that point, I began to cover the video game business continually for other outlets and wrote two books on the making of Microsoft's Xbox business. In 2008, I joined VentureBeat, a tech

Joe: I was hooked the moment I played the first Atari Pong console when I was seven years old, mesmerized by the concept of interacting with the images on my TV screen instead of just passively watching them, even if it was just a one-color blip of light at that time. This led to a lifetime of embracing technology and finding ways to develop my passion into a career. I majored in contemporary American history in college and served as editor of the student newspaper for three years. I began working at the magazine *Electronic Gaming Monthly* in 1991 and worked my way up from entry-level assistant editor to become editorial director of the entire group, responsible for five monthly magazines and several one-shot publications. Ziff-Davis acquired us in 1997 and I remained editorial director of the Ziff-Davis Game Group, where, among other stuff, I was a cofounder of the *Official U.S. PlayStation Magazine* and VideoGames.com. After nine years, I left ZD in 2000 and founded Mojo Media, where we have since become a leading supplier and packager of editorial and advertorial content for video games, sports, and other enthusiast interests for websites, magazines, and books. I wrote two books on the history of Electronic Arts and *Madden NFL Football,* and have been part of several *New York Times* nonfiction bestsellers.

so, is it really all just fun and games?

Joe: Ha! Well, in a way, yes! But there is always a trade-off when you turn a passion into your profession. It can become easy to get too absorbed in your job and the environment because your passion is real, while the rest of your life is whizzing by. I'll always love interactive entertainment, but as I get older I have fewer big blocks of uninterrupted time for gaming, so I find myself playing more iPod apps type of games because they are portable, and it's easier to jump in and out of the game.

Dean: I don't review games on a regular basis. Rather, I review games occasionally. But I write about the business of video games almost every day. It's not easy, because the video game business has become a worldwide industry with many different pieces. The tentacles range from iPhone games to hardcore console games to free web games. All of it is constantly changing. I don't get to spend as much time as I'd like playing games and relaxing. Often, I find that I have to play games that I ordinarily wouldn't choose myself, for the sake of understanding a new part of the business. It's hard work and comes with a lot of challenges.

John: The bulk of my work is actually writing. I travel to game studios and interview the creators of the biggest games out there. I do play games, but most of my time is spent writing about them. I also spend a lot of time these days filming interviews for web-based video game stories.

what classes or extracurricular activities at school helped prepare you for this job?

Dean: I took one computer science class, but that is outdated and it never proved useful to me. I think it was really important that I learned how to be a journalist, which involves collecting facts and writing fast. That's the backbone of my job as a video game business writer. But I also have to play games to understand and write about them.

Joe: Working for my college newspaper provided the most practical experience and had a big influence on my career path. I was also fortunate enough to have a few great teachers and mentors along my way to earning a B.A. in history. That, combined with a passion for playing video games, helped inform my decision to try and somehow get a job in the video games industry, even if it meant starting at the bottom.

John: As an undergrad, I majored in journalism but switched to English writing in my first year. I was already writing for the *Washington Post* at that point, so what I learned in class was reinforced on the job. The key advice I have is to join the school newspaper. I was the editor in chief of my high school paper and stuck with my college paper throughout my undergrad and grad school years. That really opened a lot of doors for me. Also, this was before blogs. There are so many more opportunities for kids today to get involved in games.

Any advice for kids thinking about starting out today?

Dean: I believe that youngsters should get practice writing their own reviews and publishing them on their own blogs. There are fewer obstacles than ever to publishing your work, so take advantage of that

Focus on continuous improvement, read the columns of people you admire, and decipher how they put those columns together. Repeat that over and over. Eventually, you can show your blog posts to potential employers and get freelance or part-time writing gigs. You should also find ways to seek out classes on journalism or writing, and pursue internships with websites or newspapers. You can be an opinionated reviewer, but you'll set yourself apart from the crowd if you're a talented journalist.

John: With the print magazine and newspaper industry in dire financial trouble, the Internet has become the main hub for video game coverage. The best advice for aspiring writers is to get your name out there by blogging. A lot of outlets also accept free content. Once you have a good collection of your work out there, you can use those links to try to get a job in the industry. But it is a much harder nut to crack today than even ten years ago.

Joe: It's all good to think big, but don't expect to be a home-run hitter right off the bat. Hitting singles and doubles and taking small steps at the outset of your career is fine, so be committed, stay focused, and be prepared to grind, grind, grind. The industry will continue to expand and specialize, so whether you end up working on, or writing about, iPod apps games, blockbuster console titles like *Gears of War*, Wii Fit software, or space simulations for NASA, there will be more opportunities in the future than there are today, so try a lot of different stuff, figure out what you really like, and start reaching for it now! ■

Game school?!

DigiPen: School for Games

One way to work in the game industry is to attend a school that specializes in teaching students how to develop games. The most famous of these colleges is the DigiPen Institute of Technology, the first school in North America to offer a bachelor's degree in game development.

In the late 1980s, when video games were just starting to gain popularity, DigiPen was a production company that specialized in creating animations and simulations. DigiPen's founder and president, Claude Comair, recognized the need for more qualified personnel, and so he contacted the president of Nintendo in 1990 to see where they were getting their staff. They discovered a mutual concern about finding skilled developers, and so, with input from Nintendo, DigiPen designed the first bachelor's degree in game programming.

Today, DigiPen has campuses around the globe. The U.S. campus, which grew from a small class of 30 to almost 900 students, is located in Redmond, Washington, and is surrounded by more than 70 game studios including companies such as Nintendo, Microsoft, Bungie, Valve, and Sony Online Entertainment.

Programs at DigiPen

A school that specializes in creating games? Sure, it *sounds* awesome, but it's hard work creating games, and so is going to school to learn how to do it. Students learn the skills necessary to create the next generation of games—the same games that you hope to enjoy five or more years down the road. That's serious business!

DigiPen's degrees cover almost every aspect of game development—from design, to art assets placed in the game, to the programming codes that make a game function. Each program is intense and rigorous.

Real-Time Interactive Simulation

DigiPen's most popular degree program is its Bachelor of Science in real-time interactive simulation (R.T.I.S.). It is a computer science degree in which students learn to program every aspect of a video game from the ground up.

In the R.T.I.S. program, students make increasingly complex video games each year as part of their curriculum. They start with a simple text-based game during their first year, and then they move on to a 2-D scrolling game. In their third and fourth years, they are creating 3-D games with networking and realistic graphics, artificial intelligence, and physics.

Computer Engineering

In DigiPen's computer engineering (C.E.) program, students learn to design and develop the hardware and systems that games are played on. Instead of focusing on telling the computer what they want it to do, the C.E. students learn to design the systems

on which the software runs. Students in the C.E. program have created everything from mobile phones to operating systems to handheld game systems to their own consoles. One group of students even got to intern at Nintendo, where they worked on some of the technology for the Wii remotes.

Production Animation

DigiPen's Bachelor of Fine Arts (B.F.A.) in production animation prepares students to become professional artists. The graduates of this program learn to apply their skills in any type of visual arts profession, whether it is in the games industry or

movie industry or for the web, commercials, or television shows. The B.F.A. students learn to create everything, including conceptual artwork; art assets for games, such as character designs, props, textures, and environments; feature animations in 2-D and 3-D; and cinematic cut scenes.

Game Design

DigiPen's game design (G.D.) students have the difficult job of learning how to make a game fun. DigiPen's G.D. students must combine knowledge from a wide variety of subjects, including the arts, humanities and social sciences, and computer science to effectively create a compelling experience for players.

Because games are a unique entertainment medium that combines visuals, audio, interaction, and intellect, G.D. students learn to incorporate art for visual design elements, including color, lighting, and architecture, and the placement of objects throughout

the game. They draw on engineering skills for programming scripts that trigger enemy behaviors and drive game play.

Finally, because games draw on subjects of all types, such as history, mythology, science fiction, and others, G.D. students have a wide exposure to social sciences to help them with character development, level design, and story lines.

How to Prepare for a Career in the Game Industry

So you've decided that you want to work in video games, but you're not sure how to get on a good path. According to Angela Kugler, director of admissions at DigiPen, there are actually a number of things that you can start doing now to prepare yourself.

"If you're interested in learning how to program or become a software or computer engineer, you should consider taking courses in mathematics and computer science; creating computer programs, machines, or inventions at home; enrolling in a game

programming camp or workshop, such as DigiPen's ProjectFun workshops or online clubs (which are open to students in fifth grade and up); or getting involved in First Robotics competitions," she advises. "And don't forget to practice your math, science, and problem-solving skills, such as puzzles. This knowledge will be essential for your success as a game programmer or computer engineer.

"If game design is your passion, you probably already stay up late coming up with your own ideas for levels, designs, games, environments, and characters. If not, start now by designing role-playing games, board games, or any other type of game and getting feedback on them. You can also take this a step further by analyzing existing games and identifying what makes them fun or how you could improve upon them.

"Finally, if you know you want to be an artist or animator, start practicing now by taking as many art courses as possible. It's best to start with traditional art courses, such as drawing,

painting, and sculpture, before diving into any digital art courses where you use the computer; however, you can certainly start familiarizing yourself with the technology that digital artists use today. As you progress through your art classes during high school, set aside some of the work that you think best represents your skills, as you'll want to include those in your art portfolio down the road."

And, of course, if you know now that you'd like to attend a school like DigiPen, there are steps you can take. Check the admissions requirements for the school of your choice—that way, you can make sure to take the right English, math, science, and art classes at your high school to prepare yourself. And build up your portfolio so it's ready to go when it's application time. Also, ask your art and computer teachers for letters of recommendation at the end of each school year. All of that looks impressive to any admissions committee! ■

Job Glossary

There is a wide variety of creative jobs requiring different skill sets in the video games industry. From music to motion capture, from alpha to beta testing, there are many different jobs and careers you can begin preparing for now. While the constant march of technology means that roles are always evolving and sometimes the line between jobs becomes blurred, the occupations listed below include many of the traditional gigs you will encounter in the industry.

According to Marc Mencher, game industry talent agent and president of GamerRecruiter, "Our industry has been in a hiring war for several years. There is just not enough technical talent to fill the needs of the North American market, let alone the worldwide game development community. The U.S. Bureau of Labor Statistics predicts that high-tech careers will thrive in the decade ending in 2012. They predict that software design jobs will grow by 54.6 percent and publishing jobs will grow by 67.9 percent."

2-D Conceptual Artist

Among the few artists in video game production who create physical pieces of art, 2-D concept artists are especially important in the early stages of a game. They draw out characters and scenes for the other artists to base their designs on, storyboard video cut scenes, and sometimes even create load screens and manual art.

2-D Texture Artist

Even as games become more and more 3-D oriented, the 2-D texture artist retains an important position in the art design of a game. Creating the walls, textures, landscapes, and even faces of characters, 2-D texture artists are responsible for a great deal of a title's realism.

3-D Character Animator

Once the game characters have been designed, it's time to make sure they move the way they are supposed to: People need to walk and run realistically, animals need to have the proper gait, and machines need to move robotically. It's up to the 3-D character animators to create realistic movements, either by hand or by using motion capture technology.

3-D Character Builder

Starting with a piece of concept art or a character from a licensed story, the 3-D character builders are responsible for designing the different animals, machines, people, and creatures in a game. Working closely with the other artists and the programming staff, it's their job to turn epic heroes and villains into moving beings.

3-D Cut Scene Artist

This is a perfect field for an artist with a background or interest in animation and film production, as 3-D cut scene artists work from storyboards to create the video cut scenes in a game. With lighting, production, voice, music, and many other variables to focus on, these artists work as a team to make movie-quality scenes within the game.

3-D Model Builder (objects)

Object specialists have very rewarding and very focused jobs—designing the objects within a game, from weapons to furniture to vehicles and even buildings. They must be goal oriented, knowing when an object has just the right amount of detail for the game it is in while also understanding the real-life intricacies of the object they've built.

Art Director

To become an art director, an artist needs to know just about everything there is about game-production, from 3-D mapping to character design. Art directors oversee the art staff, making sure the right people are in the right jobs and keeping everything coordinated. Troubleshooting problems and keeping artists focused is a big responsibility, and it's up to the art director to make sure everything goes smoothly.

Art Technician

All-purpose troubleshooters as well as important for keeping a design team up to date on the latest technologies, art technicians need to have boundless energy and an eye for efficiency. As they are commonly responsible for purchasing and maintaining the hardware and software the art team uses, art technicians need to be on the cutting edge of technology.

Associate Producer

The tasks of the associate producer (AP) change depending on the game he or she is working on and who the producer is, but the basic role of the job is one of support. APs help the producer manage the project while also filtering ideas from staff and the public. Normally an AP is focused on interfacing with the testing department and localizing the game for foreign markets.

Audio Programmer and Engineer

As games become bigger and more detailed and require more dynamic sounds, the jobs of audio programmers and engineers have become bigger and bigger. They work with the composer and writers to figure out how to synthesize sounds and music as well as implement them within the game, and their responsibilities can range from the smallest of noises to the thematic crescendos of a game climax.

Composer / Sound Engineer or Designer

Every game needs to have its backing soundtrack, and the composer is the person who gives a title its score. Whether it is sweeping classical strings for a dramatic moment or pulsing techno-pop to get the blood moving, every game needs to have the right musical accompaniment. Composers work much like film composers, selecting music to put in the game or writing the music themselves. Plus, think of all the sounds that go into a game that aren't music. There can be footsteps, voices, explosions, swords clashing, leaves rustling, and thousands of other details that go into a game's audio. Sound engineers and designers are responsible for bringing these sounds to life within the game, working with programmers to give every moment its sound.

Engine / Tools Programmer

The engine of a game is like its brain. Engine and tools programmers have very important roles in the production of video games. First, they are responsible for the code base that a game is built on, making it imperative that they be expert programmers. They also must have an understanding of the roles of other programmers, artists, and even level designers working on a project, since they create easy-to-use tools for nontechnical folks who need to be able to use the engine to make the rest of the game.

Executive Producer / Producer

Filling one of the toughest and most rewarding jobs in video games, producers have to wear several different hats at once. They are in charge of keeping a game on task, budgeting, and scheduling the project while making sure that the team members are kept happy and working efficiently. Producers represent the game and the people who work on it, putting in long hours to make sure the project is done the right way.

Game Designer / Lead Designer

Game designers work with just about every member of a game project. Designers collaborate with testers and programmers to make sure every game is all it can be, organizing all of the different elements to follow an overall plan for the game. The designer of a game is both a visionary and an effective team leader. It is important to make sure the people on the design team are working toward the same goal; the lead designer coordinates their efforts and takes on the role of decision maker along with the producer.

Game Writer

Just like their counterparts in Hollywood, game writers are in charge of scripting the scenes of a game. They write the story within the game, adding dialogue and on-screen text to bring a game idea to life. Their work can be as wide-ranging as a novel-length story with multiple scenarios for an RPG, a play-by-play for a sports game, or a linear story for an action or adventure game.

Graphics / Special Effects Programmer

While all game programmers have to understand graphics to do their jobs, it is the job of the graphics programmer to be an expert in this domain. Bringing 3-D realism to a 2-D screen is no easy task, so the graphics programmer must be goal oriented and focused, with an artistic mind-set.

Junior Programmer

This is the perfect entry-level position for a person with programming skills and a passion for video games. Junior programmers are the people who start to bring a game concept to life. Starting with a basic understanding of programming, they are trained in specific areas such as 3-D rendering and animation, artificial intelligence (AI) development, and physics.

Lead Programmer

The head of the programming team, the lead programmer is responsible for complicated coding and decision making as well as networking with other aspects of game production, especially the writing team. Responsible for making sure all of the code from different programmers works as a single unit, the lead programmer takes many parts to make a whole.

Lead Quality Assurance Tester

The lead tester is the person in charge of assembling and managing the testing team. Working closely with the production and design teams, the lead tester creates the testing schedule and maps out what exactly needs to be tested with each version of the game. This is a technical job requiring the ability to cut code and program like a junior programmer. The testing department actually works hand in hand with the programming department to make sure the code created is stable and functional.

Level Builder

Working with the level designers, programmers, writers, and testers, the level builder has to tie many different elements together to create a cohesive world or level within a game. Stitching everything together makes the game flow the way it should, and level builders help place objects, enemies, checkpoints, and other elements in their proper places.

Level Designer

Level designers are responsible for the underpinnings of specific levels or areas of a game, and focus their efforts on the game play for portions of the project. Level designers place enemies, obstacles, puzzles, and checkpoints within their areas of expertise, providing goals and challenges for players.

Marketing and Public Relations

The marketing and public relations staffs have important jobs in the production of a game, making sure the word gets out about the title in development. They keep fans and the media saturated with screen shots and updates about the game's progress, then tout the features and greatness of the title as it nears its release.

Multiplayer Networking Programmer

As the demand for multiplayer online games has increased, so, too, has the demand for programmers to work on multiplayer networks. In addition to understanding the game and what players want, these programmers need to work with the limitations of their engines as well as the systems they are working on, while also being wary of security holes that may allow cheating or hackers.

Playability Game Tester

One of the most fun but demanding jobs in the world of video games is that of the game tester. Patience is the key virtue of testers: Their job is to play the game over and over—and over again. Sometimes they just run along a wall in a game, or one level, looking to isolate bugs and document them so the design team can fix them.

Project Manager

Similar to a producer, a project manager is more focused on business operations issues such as meeting budgets and milestone objectives so the game company is profitable. Assigning tasks and managing time are the key roles of the project manager. Often a project manager is teamed with a producer. The producer focuses on production issues, and the project manager focuses on following up with every person working on a game to make sure all departments are on task and ready to finish their assignments on time and within budget.

Sales

The sales staff is responsible for the end result of all the design team's hard work: people buying the game they've put their hearts and souls into creating. Working with retail outlets, websites, and other distributors, salespeople help get the game in the store and then into gamers' hands. They help place displays in stores and keep the hype in motion after a game is released.